Ladybirds Up Close

Greg Pyers

www.raintreepublishers.co.uk
Visit our website to find out more information about **Raintree** books.

To order:
☎ Phone 44 (0) 1865 888112
📄 Send a fax to 44 (0) 1865 314091
💻 Visit the Raintree Bookshop at **www.raintreepublishers.co.uk** to browse our catalogue and order online.

First published 2005 by Heinemann Library
a division of Harcourt Education Australia,
18–22 Salmon Street, Port Melbourne Victoria 3207 Australia
(a division of Reed International Books Australia Pty Ltd,
ABN 70 001 002 357).
Visit the Heinemann Library website at
www.heinemannlibrary.com.au

Published in Great Britain by Raintree,
Halley Court, Jordan Hill, Oxford OX2 8EJ,
part of Harcourt Education
Raintree is a registered trademark of Harcourt Education Ltd.

ℝ A Reed Elsevier company

© Reed International Books Australia Pty Ltd 2005

09 08 07 06 05
10 9 8 7 6 5 4 3 2 1

Editorial: Anne McKenna, Carmel Heron
Design: Kerri Wilson, Stella Vassiliou
Photo research: Legend Images, Wendy Duncan
Production: Tracey Jarrett
Illustration: Rob Mancini

Typeset in Officina Sans 19/23 pt
Film separations by Digital Imaging Group (DIG), Melbourne
Printed and bound in Hong Kong and China by South China
Printing Company Ltd.

The paper used to print this book comes from sustainable
resources.

National Library of Australia Cataloguing-in-Publication data:

Pyers, Greg.
    Ladybirds up close.

    Includes index.
    For primary school students.
    ISBN 1 74070 232 8.

    1. Ladybugs – Juvenile literature. I. Title.
    (Series: Minibeasts up close).

595.769

Acknowledgements
The publisher would like to thank the following for permission
to reproduce photographs: APL/Ravo Images/Glen Ravenscroft:
p. **28**; Auscape/John Cancalosi: p. **27**, /Jean-Jacques Etienne-
Bios: p. **8**, /Pascal Goetgheluck: p. **14**, /C. Andrew Henley:
pp. **10, 18, 19**, /OSF/Paulo de Oliveira: p. **15**; © Dennis Kunkel
Microscopy, Inc.: p. **12**; Lochman Transparencies/Jiri Lochman:
p. **6**; Dr. Russell F. Mizell: p. **29**; photolibrary.com: pp. **13, 20,
21, 24, 25**, /Animals Animals: p. **7**, /SPL: pp. **4, 11, 26**;
© Paul Zborowski: pp. **5, 22, 23**.

Cover photograph of a seven spot ladybird reproduced with
permission of photolibrary.com/SPL/C. Nuridsayn & M. Perrenou.

Every attempt has been made to trace and acknowledge
copyright. Where an attempt has been unsuccessful, the
publisher would be pleased to hear from the copyright owner
so any omission or error can be rectified.

Contents

Words that are printed in bold, **like this**, are explained in the glossary on page 31.

Amazing ladybirds!

Have you ever seen a ladybird? Perhaps you have seen one climbing up a plant stem. Maybe one has rested on your finger before opening its wings and flying away. When you look at them up close, ladybirds really are amazing animals.

If you look closely, you may see a ladybird in a garden.

What are ladybirds?

Ladybirds are **beetles**.
They are small, round
and brightly coloured.
Most ladybirds are red
or yellow, with black spots.
But some are brown, and
some have white spots. Some
ladybirds have seven spots, others
have fourteen or twenty-two spots.

Like all beetles, ladybirds are insects.
Insects have six legs and no bones inside
their bodies. Instead, their bodies have a
hard, waterproof skin. This skin is called
an **exoskeleton**.

This **species**, or
kind, of ladybird
has no spots.

Different names

In North America, ladybirds are
known as 'ladybugs' or 'ladybeetles'.

Where do ladybirds live?

Ladybirds live in all parts of the world, except Antarctica. Like all insects, ladybirds are most often seen when the weather is warm. But they can survive very cold winters.

Habitat

A **habitat** is a place where an animal lives. Different **species** of ladybirds have different habitats. In Britain, the orange ladybird lives only in forests. This is because it eats the **fungus** that grows on tree trunks.

This type of ladybird lives in rainforests.

The water ladybird finds its food in wet, muddy places. The striped ladybird finds its food in pine forests. The two-spot ladybird lives in many habitats. This is because the insects it eats also live in many habitats.

Two-spot ladybirds are often found on tree trunks.

Ladybird body parts

A ladybird's body has three main parts. These are the head, the **thorax** and the **abdomen** (<u>ab</u>-da-men).

The head

A ladybird's head is much smaller than its thorax and abdomen. The head has two feelers called **antennae** (an-<u>ten</u>-ay), two eyes and a mouth. The mouth has strong, biting jaws called **mandibles**.

abdomen

thorax

head

antenna

The thorax

A ladybird's wings and all six of its legs are attached to the thorax. There are strong muscles inside the thorax. These are needed to work the wings and legs.

The abdomen

Food is digested in the ladybird's abdomen. This means the food is broken down into tiny pieces. In females, eggs are produced in the abdomen.

Under cover

The ladybird's abdomen is usually completely covered by the wings. The abdomen can be seen only when the ladybird spreads its wings to take off.

Mouthparts and eating

Most ladybirds eat small insects called aphids. Aphids are easy to catch because they move very slowly. When aphids are feeding, they do not move at all.

This ladybird is eating an aphid. Ladybirds also eat other small insects, such as scale insects.

Jaws

Ladybirds have strong jaws, or **mandibles**, which can easily crush the soft bodies of aphids. In its lifetime, a ladybird may eat more than 5000 aphids.

Before they become adults, ladybirds are **larvae**. Larvae are tiny grubs, but they have strong jaws. One ladybird larva may eat 400 aphids before it begins to change into an adult.

Palps

A ladybird has **palps** on each side of its mouth. They help to move the food to the mouth.

mandible

palp

In this close-up photo you can see that the ladybird's palps are shaped like fingers.

Seeing and sensing

Ladybirds can see, taste and smell. But not in the same way we do.

Eyes

A ladybird has two **compound eyes**. Each compound eye is made up of thousands of very small eyes. Each small eye faces in a slightly different direction. Together, the small eyes give a ladybird an excellent view to the front, side and back.

This close-up photo shows how the small eyes of a compound eye fit tightly together.

Antennae

A ladybird uses its **antennae**, or feelers, to smell. This helps the ladybird find its **prey** or a mate. The ladybird also uses its antennae to touch and taste.

The antennae can **sense** air movement. A sudden breeze may warn the ladybird that a **predator** is near. It might warn that a strong wind is coming, and that it should hold on tight or seek shelter.

Palps

A ladybird uses its **palps** to taste its food.

antenna

This ladybird is using its antennae to sense the air.

Wings and flying

Ladybirds have two pairs of wings. But only one pair is used to fly.

Wings

The two front wings are really wing cases. They are hard and thick. They protect the rear pair of wings.

A ladybird's rear wings are its flying wings. They are thin, soft and clear. When a ladybird is not flying, these wings are safely hidden beneath the wing cases.

wing case

A ladybird's wing cases are what you see when you look at its back.

Flying

Ladybirds fly to get away from **predators**, such as spiders. Another reason is to search for food. When a ladybird prepares to fly, it climbs to a high point on a plant. It folds its wing cases back, then unfolds its flying wings. These wings beat so fast they appear as a blur, and then the ladybird takes off.

wing case

flying wing

This ladybird is about to land on a plant stem covered in aphids.

Fast wingbeats

When flying, a ladybird's wings beat up and down between 80 and 90 times a second.

Inside a ladybird

Ladybirds have blood that is clear, and a heart that is a tube.

Blood

A ladybird's blood moves through the spaces in its body. The blood travels from the head, through the **thorax** and into the **abdomen**. From there, the heart pumps it forward again.

How do ladybirds get air?

A ladybird does not breathe through its mouth. It gets air into its body through tiny holes called **spiracles** (<u>spi</u>-ra-kels). These are on each side of a ladybird's body.

The brain

A ladybird's brain gets information that it **senses** through its **antennae**, eyes and **palps**. It sends messages to the rest of the ladybird's body about what to do.

What happens to food?

When a ladybird swallows, pieces of food pass along a tube and into the stomach. As the food moves, it is broken down to release **nutrients**. A ladybird needs nutrients to stay alive. Waste passes out through the anus.

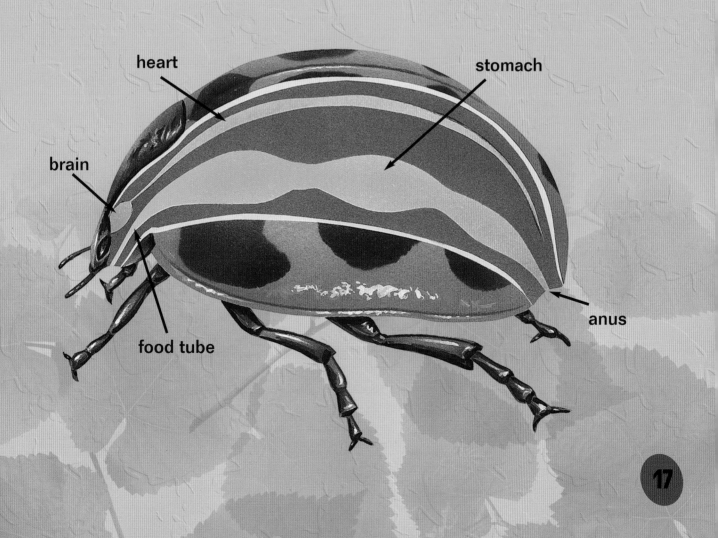

heart

stomach

brain

food tube

anus

Eggs and larvae

After she **mates** with a male, a female ladybird lays her eggs in the warm weather of spring and summer.

Eggs

The female lays between 20 and 30 eggs. She lays them on a plant where there are many aphids. The eggs stick to the leaf or stem in a tightly packed group. After a week, the eggs begin to hatch.

This ladybird has just laid her eggs on a leaf.

Ladybird larvae climb
up and down stems
and leaves looking
for aphids to eat.

Larvae

Tiny grubs break through
the thin eggshells and
crawl from the eggs. These
grubs are the ladybird **larvae**. The
larvae eat their empty eggshells and then go
in search of aphids to eat. A ladybird larva
eats about 30 aphids a day.

A larva does not look like an adult ladybird.
It has six legs, but it is a different colour and
has no wings. Its body has stiff hairs on it.

Becoming an adult

The **larva** grows very fast. It soon outgrows its own skin. The skin splits and the larva crawls out in a new, bigger skin. This is called **moulting**. The larva keeps eating and will moult several more times.

Pupa

Three weeks after hatching, the larva attaches its back end to a stem. Its skin then splits and falls off. What is left stuck to the stem is a **pupa**. An adult ladybird is growing inside the pupa.

This ladybird pupa is attached to a plant stem.

The adult

About a week later, the pupa's skin splits and an adult ladybird breaks out. It is soft and pale. It stays still on the stem while its **exoskeleton** hardens. In an hour it will be able to fly. In a day, its adult colours and spots will appear.

This California ladybird has just crawled out of its pupa.

Protection

A ladybird needs to protect itself from **predators**.

Ladybird defences

A red and black ladybird is very easy to see as it walks up a green stem. However, predators learn that brightly coloured insects have stings or taste awful. Ladybird **larvae** and adults do not have stings, but many of them have a horrible taste and smell. Once a bird, a spider or a frog has tasted a ladybird, it will leave other ladybirds alone.

With their bright colours, ladybirds are very easy to see.

Sometimes, when a predator is near, a ladybird will roll onto its back and pretend to be dead. Many predators will not attack an insect that does not move.

Larvae defences

Ladybird **larvae** have strong jaws that can be used to fight off small predators, such as shieldbugs.

A ladybird can also tuck its head under the front of its **thorax**. Its feet act like suction cups. They hold the ladybird tightly to a stem or leaf so that a predator cannot pull it off.

This ladybird has tucked its head in for protection.

23

Ladybirds in winter

When winter comes, there are no aphids. It is also too cold for ladybirds to move. So how do they survive?

Safe places

As the weather becomes cold, ladybirds find places that are dry and sheltered from the wind. This may be deep in the **leaf litter** of a forest, under hedges or inside hollow logs.

These seven-spot ladybirds are sheltering together under a leaf for the winter.

Places to shelter

Ladybirds that live in pine forests may shelter among the pine needles high in a tree. Some ladybirds often shelter in cracks in the bark of tree trunks. Ladybirds also shelter in buildings such as garden sheds.

Different **species** of ladybirds may join together to shelter in groups.

Groups

Ladybirds often shelter in large groups. There may be hundreds or thousands of ladybirds in the same place. Some ladybirds return to the same place each winter.

By huddling in large groups, ladybirds are also using their own bodies as shelter. A **chemical** in their bodies keeps them from freezing. Ladybirds can even survive under snow when they are in these large groups.

Migrating ladybirds

The convergent ladybird of the USA travels, or **migrates**, many kilometres every year.

Getting warmer

In spring, in the valleys of central California, convergent ladybird **larvae** feed on aphids. By summer, these larvae will have become adults. But soon after, when it gets really hot, the number of aphids falls. If the ladybirds stayed in the valleys, they would starve.

This convergent ladybird is eating aphids.

Time to move

In late summer, convergent ladybirds gather in huge **swarms**. There may be millions of ladybirds in a single swarm. They fly 80 kilometres (50 miles) or more to the mountains. It is cooler there and there is enough food to last until autumn.

Getting colder

As winter comes, aphids disappear. The ladybirds rest over the cold months ahead. The following spring, the ladybirds **mate** and migrate back into the valleys. There will be aphids feeding on crops by then.

In winter, convergent ladybirds form large groups and shelter beneath logs and **leaf litter**.

27

Ladybirds and us

Ladybirds are a sign of a good season for crops because they eat insects that damage crops.

Farmers' friends

Two Australian ladybird species were released in California more than 100 years ago. It was hoped they would control an insect pest, the cottony cushion scale insect. This insect attacks orange and lemon trees. The ladybirds saved the Californian fruit trees from disaster.

Most people like ladybirds.

Pests

When ladybirds seek winter shelter inside houses, they can be a real pest. It the ladybirds are disturbed, they give off a bad smell. In Kentucky, in the USA, thousands of Asian ladybirds may enter a single house to shelter for the winter. This ladybird was brought to Kentucky to control aphids.

Bean beetle

The Mexican bean **beetle** is a pest ladybird. It is brownish yellow with black spots. It feeds on bean leaves and pods.

These Asian ladybirds were removed from a house in the USA, where they went to shelter for winter.

Find out for yourself

You may be able to find some ladybirds in a garden. Look among the leaves of shrubs. If you see aphids, ladybirds are almost certain to be around. Maybe you will see ladybird **larvae** eating the aphids.

Books to read

Living Nature: Insects, Angela Royston (Chrysalis Children's Books, 2003)

Looking at Minibeasts: Ladybirds and Beetles, Sally Morgan (Belitha Press, 2001)

Using the Internet

Explore the Internet to find out more about ladybirds. Websites can change, so do not worry if the links below no longer work. Use a search engine, such as www.yahooligans.com or www.internet4kids.com, and type in a keyword such as 'ladybird', or the name of a particular ladybird **species**.

Websites

http://www.ladybird-survey.pwp.blueyonder.co.uk/londonla.htm
This site has photos and information about British ladybirds.

http://www.uoguelph.ca/~samarsha/lady-beetles.htm
This site has photos and information about North American ladybirds.

Glossary

abdomen last of the three main sections of an insect

antenna (plural: antennae) feeler on an insect's head

beetle insect with hard wing covers

chemical substance

compound eye eye made up of many parts

exoskeleton hard outside skin of an insect

fungus (plural: fungi) plant-like living thing that feeds on dead plants and animals

habitat place where an animal lives

larva (plural: larvae) stage in a ladybird's life between egg and adult

leaf litter dead and rotting leaves on the forest floor

mandible jaw

mate when a male and a female come together to produce young

migrate move from one place to another, often over a long distance

moult when a growing insect splits open its exoskeleton and climbs out of it; many insects need to moult so they can grow

nutrients parts of food that are important for an animal's health

palp finger-like part of a ladybird's mouth

predator animal that kills and eats other animals

prey animal that is caught and eaten by other animals

pupa (plural: pupae) stage in a ladybird's life between larva and adult

sense how an animal knows what is going on around it, such as by seeing, hearing or smelling

species type or kind of animal

spiracle tiny air hole

swarm large number of ladybirds flying together

thorax chest part of an insect

Index